ONE HUNDRED

Charting a Course Past 100 in Sunday School

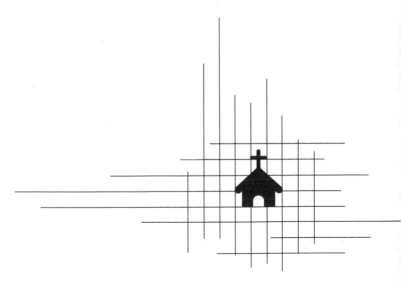

David Francis and Michael Kelley

David Francis

Director of Sunday School at LifeWay. Member of the Minister of Education tribe. Preschool Sunday School teacher with wife, Vickie. Dad to 3 sons. Grandaddy to 5. Author of 13 books. 12 are free on iTunes or at *LifeWay.com/DavidFrancis*.

Michael Kelley

Director of Groups Ministry at LifeWay. Father of three. Husband of one, Jana. Church elder. Author of *Wednesdays were Pretty Normal, Faith Limps, Holy Vocabulary, Hard Sayings of Jesus,* and *Boring.* Blogger (*MichaelKelleyMinistries.com*).

ISBN 978 1 4300 6372 1
Item 005791349

By completing a study of this book, you can receive course credit in the Christian Growth Study Plan. For more information, visit *LifeWay.com/CGSP*.

Dewey decimal classification: 268.0
Subject headings: SUNDAY SCHOOLS/RELIGIOUS EDUCATION

Unless otherwise noted, all Scripture quotations are taken from the HCSB, © 1999, 2000, 2002, 2003, 2009 by Holman Bible Publishers. Used by permission.

Printed in the United States of America

Groups Ministry
LifeWay Church Resources
One LifeWay Plaza
Nashville, TN 37234-0175

Contents

One ... Hundred 4

Understand the Numbers 9

Acknowledge the Power of One 13

Encourage Four Great Expectations 15

Expect New People Every Week, Expect a Great Bible Study Experience Every Week, Expect to Follow Up Aggressively, Expect People to Say Yes

Develop Six Dynamics of a Culture of Invitation 29

Invigorate, Incorporate, Intercede, Invest, Invite, Involve

Act on Five Proven Steps to Growth 36

Dream, Declare, Develop, Determine, Deploy

Embrace Four Foundational Principles 39

Care for Every Person, Open Groups, Open Enrollment, The Irreducible Law of Kingdom Growth

Divide the Work around Four Age Groups 51

Preschool, Kids, Students, Adults

Balance Three Dimensions 53

Disciple Making, Community Building, Culture Impacting

Take it to the Next Level 56

Class, Community, Commission

"One" Revisited 61

Endnotes 63

One...

One person. One baby. One preschooler. One second grader. One middle school boy. One high school girl. One college student. One young couple. One senior saint. One man mowing the grass on Saturday. One deacon arriving early to unlock the doors. One smocked lady in her place in the nursery, bright smile ready to greet a new little one—whether one comes or not. One couple using the resources they have to create the best experience they can for a room of kids. Another one with donuts in hand eagerly circles up with the youth group. One teacher prepared to lead an (or the) adult class in a discussion of the day's Bible passage. One class that leads the way in growth. One pastor called by God to serve and lead this flock as shepherd-teacher. One enthusiastic person who comes alongside him as Sunday School Director. Smaller churches know the value of one!

...Hundred

100. One hundred times one. Half of Southern Baptist churches (over 20,000 churches) will host between one and 100 people in worship and Bible study next Sunday. In another 40 percent of SBC churches, between 100 and 200 will gather for fellowship and discipleship. A church that averages over 200 in Sunday School is in the top 10 percent. They are "big" churches. So what's another adjective for the smaller church? How about "normal"? Averaging less than 100 in attendance is remarkably normal!

Good News for Smaller Churches

Everybody doesn't want to go to a mega-church! The reality is most people aren't thinking about going to any church. So they go to the big church because they got a fancy postcard in the mail? Actually, no. Or because they saw the scrolling message on the fancy sign? Again, not really. Those things may have created an awareness of the church for them. Most people will not respond to those things alone. What they will respond to is an invitation. An invitation from someone they admire or trust who talks enthusiastically about how his or her church is making a difference in his or her life. An invitation that leads to a positive experience on that trial visit. An experience that is followed by a gracious invitation to come back again. A church of any size can do that. The advantage for a smaller church is that the first visit to the church is not like going to the super-center. It's more like going to the neighborhood market. It's a lot less intimidating. In this book, we will learn how to make it even less intimidating.

Congregational Self-esteem

Many people faithfully attend churches they never invite anybody to visit. Why? Partly because the congregation has low self-esteem. Acting on some of the ideas in this book will help you feel great about your church. Some people think it is music or architecture or something else that attracts people to a church. It's not. Churches grow for one main reason: people invite other people. And people only invite other people when they feel good about what they are inviting them to. How would you rate your congregational self-esteem?

Conversations

Tom Peters and Robert Waterman have long emphasized that excellence is not about doing any one thing 100 times better, but doing 100 things a little better.[1] The purpose of this book is to provoke conversations about the 100 little things that can be done better. Conversations allow people to think and process thoughts. The opportunity to process thoughts through conversation can bring people a sense of agreement about actions that produce incremental positive changes in the life of a church. And with each improvement, the guest experience is better, the congregation's self-esteem goes up, and members invite people more naturally.

...on a Path Past 100

If your pastor has given you this book, it is because he believes you can contribute to a conversation among members of a church that
- *averages less than 100 in Sunday School attendance, and*
- *wants to move beyond the 100 barrier, and*
- *intends to provide an excellent Bible study experience for every one—on both sides of 100.*

What might it look like for a church to reach 50, then 75, then 100, then 150? Even 200? Let's look at a typical example.

50	75	100	150	200	
Preschool	Babies-Twos	Babies-Twos	Babies	Babies	
			Ones-Twos	Ones-Twos	
	Threes-Kindergarten	Threes-Kindergarten	Threes-Pre-K	Threes	
				Pre-K	
			Kindergarten	Kindergarten	
Kids	Grades 1-3	Grades 1-3	Grades 1-2	Grade 1	S p e c i a l B u d d i e s
				Grade 2	
			Grades 3-4	Grade 3	
	Grades 4-6	Grades 4-6		Grade 4	
			Grades 5-6	Grade 5	
				Grade 6	
Students	Students	Middle School	MS Boys	7-8 Boys	
			MS Girls	7-8 Girls	
		High School	High School	HS Boys	
				HS Girls	
Adults	Adults	Young Adults	Young Adults	College/Career	
				Nearly/Newlywed	
				Young Married	
			Special Needs	Special Needs	
		Adults			
			Parents	Parents	
			Empty Nesters	Empty Nesters	
Senior Adults	Senior Adult Women	Senior Adult Women	Senior Adult Women	Senior Adult Women	
				Senior Adult Women	
	Senior Adult Men	Senior Adult Men	Senior Adult Men	Senior Adult Men	
		Senior Adult Coed	Senior Adult Coed	Senior Adult Coed	

We are going to explore some of the key numbers next. We need to state one now. The example on the facing page is built on it. Simply stated, attendance will seldom exceed a class:attendance ratio of 1:10.

A Foundation for 50

At a minimum, any size Sunday School should have four classes, one each for preschoolers, elementary age kids, students (youth), and adults. That foundation, plus an additional adult class, is probably sufficient to sustain an attendance of up to 50. For over 10,000 SBC churches, getting to 50 is the next goal.

Beating the Average at 75

What would it take to be above average in attendance? Maybe three more classes. What changes in the example? What are some other configurations that might take a church past 75? Another significant thing happens at about 75: church budget approaches $100,000. Ten or eleven classes may be enough to put a church into triple-digits.

From "Broadly Graded" to "Narrowly Graded"

Something significant happens at 150. You have the opportunity to choose curriculum that is more targeted. Perhaps more significant, a church can rarely sustain an attendance above 150 without adding vocational staff.

Into the Top Ten Percent

We get sort of tickled when someone from a church of 200 or more tells us, "We're just a little church." A church with 200 in Sunday School is larger than 90 percent of churches. It likely has at least 20 classes. It has begun to target more precise groups of people. At 200 and probably way before, the church can provide Sunday School for kids and adults with special needs. Budget giving has likely exceeded a quarter of a million dollars, plus whatever the people who only attend worship give.

Why We Focus on Sunday School Attendance

Sunday School attendance is a much more reliable gauge of church health than worship attendance. People who attend Sunday School and worship give up to six times more money than those who attend worship only.

Out of 100 people who attend worship and Sunday School, over 80 will still be active five years from now. Of 100 who attend only worship, fewer than 20 will be.

It's More than Numbers

Have you ever stood between a set of railroad tracks and looked down the rails? The tracks appear to get closer and closer to each other in the horizon. Eventually, they appear to merge together into one rail. Sunday School has two rails. One rail is numerical growth: more people being reached with the gospel. The other rail is spiritual growth: individuals being matured in Christ. Are you better at one rail than the other? Can you accelerate both numerical and spiritual growth at the same time? If you said "yes," that's the spirit of One ... Hundred.

Excellence One Class at a Time

Whether you have 4 classes or 40, the Bible study experience can be excellent in every class. There is no reason that a class for kids in a smaller church can't be just as good as one in a bigger church. Same for any other age group. The room can look just as appealing. The workers can be just as well trained. The curriculum can be just as effective. Especially if you invest in "the works." Some smaller churches decide too soon they can't afford resources like music and video and posters and activity sheets. The reality is you can't afford *not* to provide these resources. You can't afford not to outfit the rooms with the best equipment. And if you do, the Bible study experience will not only rival one at the big church; it may surpass it. More importantly, the boys and girls will have a superior discipleship experience, too. Our motivation for excellence is not to compete with the nearest mega-church. Rather, it is to effectively compete for the minds and hearts and souls of the people we are entrusted to disciple, whether we grow or not. That said, we do well to understand the numbers.

Understand the Numbers

Let's talk about some of the key numbers. You may want to put a tab on this page in case you want to refer back to it again.

150

W. L. Gore & Associates has been perpetually named as one of the top 100 companies to work for. Although it employs thousands of employees around the world, the size of each of its facilities is normally limited to 150 people. Malcolm Gladwell brought attention to this number in *Tipping Point*.[2] It is called Dunbar's Number after the Oxford anthropologist who popularized the theory. He contends that 150 is sort of a universal maximum for social groupings. He ties it to brain size, thus a maximum number of "cognitive relationships" most humans can keep up with. A company in the U.S. Army seldom exceeds 150 soldiers. Many villages around the world have about 150 residents. The examples go on and on. This fascinating topic suggests an important question: What if 150 is just sort of normal—the maximum number of people a typical pastor can effectively shepherd by himself? To move beyond that, he needs help. And the willingness not to know everything about everybody!

67

The average percent of worship attenders who also participate in Sunday School on an average Sunday in SBC churches. On a typical weekend, about 6 million people will be at church during worship and 4 million will come before or stay after worship for Sunday School. Smaller churches often have a much higher ratio. But 2:3 is the average.

150:100

Have you done the math already? An average church with 150 during worship (including preschoolers and kids elsewhere in the building) is going to have how many in Sunday School? That's right: 100. Fortunately, in smaller churches, the gap is often lower.

82 of 100 plus 8 of 50

In research findings reported by Thom Rainer in the book *High Expectations,* an analysis was made of people who had come to Christ and joined a sampling of churches five years earlier.[3] We've already mentioned this earlier, but the findings demand us to look at this more closely. Of those who attended both worship and Sunday School, 82% were still active. Of those who attended only worship, just 16% remained active. So take a church with 150 in worship: 50 who attend worship only and 100 who attend both Sunday School and worship. If the research plays out in that church, five years later, 82 of the 100 will still be around. But of those who attend only worship, only 8 of those 50 will still be there. Eight. How do these dynamics impact the way you view the importance of getting people into Sunday School?

50

The percentage of people enrolled in Sunday School who attend on any given Sunday. This 1:2 ratio has held for many decades, with fluctuations up or down rarely exceeding one percent. This percentage may vary considerably by church or by class. A normal range is 40-60%.

75

The typical church in North America will have about 75 people "in the house" on any given Sunday. Are you starting to see a pattern? 75 is half of 150. The big number is always the driver. I don't know why it is, but when churches cull non-attenders from the Sunday School roll, average attendance will eventually settle into—you guessed it—50 percent of enrollment. Yes, even if the people culled were inactive.

200

The Sunday School enrollment required in the typical church to net an average attendance of 100. What is your current enrollment?

Active Enrollment

You minister to more people than you think! You will probably be encouraged by this number. Calculate it by determining how many members attended at least once during a given month. Do you count guests? Only if they agree to enroll as members. Most will if asked. What was your active enrollment average for October or March, whichever was most recent?

20

Percentage of "churn" in the typical church. What is churn? It is the number of new people required each year for attendance to just stay even. You can count it. Just add up the number of people who no longer attend because they have dropped out, moved away, or gone to heaven. If you can, go back five years. If you don't have the records—or memories, then assume 20 percent of attendance (10 percent of enrollment). So a church that averages 60 in attendance is going to need to reach about 12 new people next year just to stay at 60.

10

The average attendance per class across age groups over time. I (David) have tested this across the country in churches of all sizes. If you will tell me how many classes you have, I can get pretty close to guessing your average attendance by multiplying by 10. Or if you'll tell me your average attendance, I can make a pretty good guess about how many classes you have by dividing by 10. Preschool classes tend to have less than 10. Adult classes tend to average a few more. But over time, the overall average will be about 10 per class.

10,000

The number of dollars a new class of 10 will add to the annual budget receipts. That is a conservative number, assuming $20 per person per week for 50 weeks. At $25 per person, the annual budget would be $125,000 when attendance reached 100. That includes the kids, who are included in the per person total. If you calculate per person giving using worship attendance, it will be lower. People who attend only worship give six times less than those who attend both worship and Sunday School.[4]

60/40

A typical ratio of attendance in adult classes and in non-adult classes in a healthy church. The 40 includes the adults working with preschoolers, kids, and students. If the second number is higher than 40, you probably have a real challenge enlisting enough leaders to teach and care for preschoolers, kids, and students. If the first number is higher than 60, you probably don't have a healthy number of preschoolers, kids, students, and their parents.

12-15

Percent of the total attendance that will be in a preschool, kids, or student class (including the adult leaders). Since you have 3 age groups, we need to multiply by 3. That's 12 times 3 or 15 times 3. So a healthy range of 36-45 percent. Or a "center cut" number of about 40 percent total in preschool, kids, and student classes.

3

Standard number of leaders for each class. Ideally, you will have a person in each class who is primarily responsible for each of the three priorities of Sunday School. An adult class can operate with one. A class for kids should never have fewer than two. Three are better, especially if two are a married couple. One of the teachers in a class for preschoolers or children will serve as the lead teacher or director. All the teachers in a kids class will also function as care group leaders. There's another more important reason why it's best to have at least a three-person team in every child's room: for the safety and security of the children and the protection of the workers.

2:1

The ratio of attendance to parking spaces almost every church needs. If you want to grow past the 100 barrier, how many parking spaces are required? How many do you need if your goal is 150? How many spaces do you have now?

2

The number of years it usually takes for an existing adult class to plateau. It will likely still continue to "cover its churn." That is, a class of ten that loses two will make up that two. But it is the rare class that gets bigger after two years. Unless, of course, it experiences a revival by doing something like committing to some of the things in this book! Seriously, some churches have not started a new class in years. It's not a failure on the part of the teacher. It's just normal.

1

There is power in one.

Acknowledge the Power of One

The Greek New Testament word for power is *dunamis*. It is the word from which we get the English word dynamic. And the word dynamite. The power of one can be positive or negative. One can propel things forward or shut things down. The latter is usually motivated by a desire to retain the power of one. The former has discovered—or is willing to discover—the joy of being a channel for the power of the Holy Spirit. I am going to assume that's the kind of power you enjoy!

One Teacher

Perhaps no one has more influence over people than Adult Sunday School teachers. If they are for something, it goes. If they oppose something, it does not—at least in that class. A path past 100 will absolutely require the support of adult teachers.

One Class

One class—dedicated to the goal—is enough to propel a church past 100 in Sunday School attendance, even if that class is acting alone. It will take a while longer, but one motivated class led by one visionary teacher can lead the way. Here's another thing about one class. Contrary to the popular myth, there is absolutely no reason that a preschool class, a kids class, a student class, or an adult class in a smaller church can't be just as great a learning experience as a similar class in a big church. In fact, there's no reason for it not to be better! The class is the foundational unit of the Sunday School. A large church just has more of them. It is just a matter of scale. Dedicated teachers equipped with great curriculum in a bright, clean, safe environment and empowered by the Holy Spirit can absolutely create a Bible study experience in a smaller church that is equal to—or better than—what happens in a big church.

One Growing Disciple

Whether we grow past 100 or not, we still have a responsibility for helping the disciples we have to grow. Jesus said a good shepherd leaves the 99 to search for the one that is lost. How did the shepherd know one sheep was missing? He counted them! This story is a perfect picture of the spirit of "One...Hundred."

One Antagonist

Just one insatiably negative person can mess all our plans up. Satan is having a heyday in too many churches of all sizes. People may attend a church or class that is out of sorts, but I'll promise you this: few of them are going to invite someone else to come watch the fight!

If you are the church antagonist, please repent or leave. But if you leave, please don't join another church. I know that sounds harsh, but this is a very serious problem in far too many churches, and is probably one of the key factors preventing us from accomplishing the Great Commission. Let's be clear. We're not talking about the person who offers occasional feedback about things that could be done better. All of us do that, and should. We're talking about the person who is consistently negative about everything. He or she has been acting the same way for a number of years, through a number of pastorates, and with a virtually inexhaustible list of grievances. The kind of person who is not happy unless he is unhappy! The kind of person also sets himself up as the grand permission giver. Why do such people even want to go to church? They usually represent a very tiny minority of the church membership, usually only one or two people who work behind the scenes to maintain power. How do these people retain their negative power in a church? Usually, it's because the new people and the nice people just leave or cower. Often the very antagonists who cause others to leave blame the church leadership—and usually the pastor specifically—for the departure. It's sick. At the very heart of all this is the desire on the part of the antagonist to stay in power no matter what. If the church grows, they reason in their warped mind, they may lose power. So the way to retain power is to keep the church small. Oh, they'll deny it's so. But it usually is.[5]

What's the solution? Serious situations may require some form of intervention. All require intercession. Something remarkable happens when people in a church start praying for their church, their pastor, their class, their teacher, and the other people in the church.

One You

One can make a difference. Will you be one of those ones? If so, here's how ...

Encourage Four Great Expectations

We tend to get what we expect. If we expect to enjoy a game or event, we typically do. If we expect the game or event to be boring, it typically is. Expectations are important when it comes to Sunday School.

1. Expect New People Every Week

Do you expect new people every week? If you do, everything is impacted. You'll be there early. You'll park away from the building to make room for guests. You'll leave the back couple of rows empty so guests can sit there if they want to. You'll scoot in from the aisle to make room for a guest. You'll do your part to help get the house ready for company. What might you do around the church or in your room that shows you're expecting company?

Reduce Clutter and Nonessential Equipment

This is a very practical thing churches of all sizes can do. It's a great place to start down a path past 100. Many rooms could hold more people if they were just cleaner and less cluttered. Preschool and children's space can be cleared of old, unsafe, or unnecessary toys and equipment. Tables in adult classes almost always limit the size of a group. Cabinets can be cleaned out or removed. Stay vigilant. Make regular "search and dispose" missions. Remove old materials from desks and shelves. Find new homes for abandoned Bibles. Remove outdated posters. Could you remove enough clutter to make space for one more person? Wayne Poling suggests carrying around a floor tile. Typically, the square foot it represents equals $100 in construction costs. How much is that old couch costing you? What are some other ways to demonstrate you're ready for company?

Signs, Signs, Everywhere a Sign!

A lot of churches could show they expect new people by simply improving the quality of the outdoor church sign. A sign says so much about the way a church feels about itself. Congregational self-esteem is the foundation of a culture of invitation. Internal signage is also important. It doesn't have to be airport or hospital quality. It just needs to be attractive and functional enough to help people get where they need to go.

The Importance of the Door

Pay special attention to the first door you expect people to walk through. And then every other door you expect them to walk through. A pastor in an Alabama church where I was speaking asked me, "After being here this morning, give me just one recommendation for making a better first impression." My response was nearly immediate: "Get a new door." The church had excellent guest parking. And signs directing guests to a fine welcome center. But the door nearest the guest parking was in ill repair. In fact, it was probably the worst door in the entire building. No one noticed much, because almost nobody used that door except guests! I recommended that the creaky, wooden door with the peeling paint be replaced with a glass door on a metal frame. It was a simple, relatively inexpensive improvement that communicates "We're expecting new people every week." And remember, the most important doors are the ones families will send their kids through.

Best Rooms for Kids

I seldom talk with a church leader who is satisfied with the number of young families his or her church is reaching. Here is a simple axiom: If you want to reach families with kids, you've got to devote the best rooms to kids. Bright rooms. Clean rooms. Well equipped rooms. With well equipped leaders. Nothing makes a more positive first impression with a parent than workers who have arrived early, set the room up with appropriate activities that invite kids to learn, turned on a music CD, and then kneel to greet a new child on his or her eye level and express how glad they are to see them. These are simple acts that make a world of difference to newcomers. Do you have great expectations that new families—with kids—will come to your church every week? Then get ready for them!

It Starts with Parking the Car

What can we do to make that very first impression a superb one for those who visit our church? Let me tell you what one church did. Briarwood is located in Cordova, Tennessee, just a short distance from the massive Bellevue Baptist Church. It was averaging about 100 in attendance when Education Pastor Steve Polk came to the church. One of the first things he did was to reserve several of the most convenient parking spaces for guests. He had signs made that read "First Time Guests." Steve enlisted a couple of men to be special greeters of these first time guests. The greeters handed each new guest an information sheet printed on brightly colored 11 x 17 paper and folded in half. And here's the best part. He began to spread the word among the members to be especially friendly to anyone with one of the very obvious information sheets! That's one of the little ways you begin to create a culture of invitation. Members will know that if they invite someone to attend, the guests will be treated well when they come.

Welcome Desk

Even in a smaller church, you need a welcome desk. Don't expect people to find their own way around. Help them complete the appropriate forms. Then escort them to their destination. If they have children, start with the youngest, the next youngest, and so forth until the adults reach their rooms. Talk along the way. Ask questions. Listen to their story. Tell things about the church building along the informal tour. "Our church building isn't big enough for all that stuff," you may protest. Guess what? It will never grow if you keep acting as if it's small.

The welcome desk should also help the guests know which Sunday School class to attend. The name of the group is important. Mr. John's class tells them who teaches the class, but the name doesn't tell them who attends the class. Use class names that are descriptive of the group and make sure everyone has at least one class that would include them.

Greet and Register All Guests

Make sure you start the process from the point the newcomer gets to your door. If a guest or new member has not provided information on a form or card, you take care of that. Fill it out for them. Approach the task conversationally. Going to church for the first time shouldn't be like going to a new doctor's office!

Nametags: Symbols of Faith that Make Connecting Easier

Nothing makes a newcomer relax more than a roomful of people wearing nametags. If you do only one thing to help people connect, do this. Make it fun, too! Everyone could print something different below their name each week, such as hometown, high school mascot, favorite sports team, favorite restaurant, age of oldest child, anniversary, birthday, and so forth. This can help members connect with one another, too.

I (David) visited Hope Fellowship Church, a new ministry in an old building in Cambridge, Massachusetts. As I entered the small foyer, I was warmly greeted by several smiling young people, perhaps students at Harvard or another university, all wearing stick-on nametags. They asked enthusiastically if I would like to make a nametag. Of course, I agreed, mainly because everyone else had one, too. Complete strangers were greeting me by name, and I was able to return the greeting in kind. I felt so comfortable! This church grew in just a couple of years from less than 20 to over 160. It is made up not only of college students, but people from the surrounding neighborhoods as well.

But remember, there is also something deeper going on here than identifying people. A nametag is a symbol of faith as well as personal identity and significance. It says, "I'm a unique and special person, and I expect to meet someone new today, maybe someone God wants me to help connect to Him."

Show Some Teeth!

My friend David Apple, a LifeWay Adult Ministry Specialist, tells a great story about a church where he was interim pastor. The church had been through some trying times, and everybody in the church and in the town where it was located knew about the problems. A lot of anger over hurt feelings simmered just beneath the emotional surface of the church services. One Sunday evening, David challenged them with what he described as the first step in a strategy to revitalize the church: SST. "Show Some Teeth!" He even suggested that gritted teeth can look like a smile from a distance! Under his interim leadership, the church experienced a revival. It began to reach people, and even began to see people saved and baptized regularly. It all started with a commitment to show some teeth!

Maintain a Simple Website

Even the smallest church needs a website. It doesn't have to be fancy. It can start with one page with the address, schedule, and phone numbers. It's easier and cheaper than you might think. Check out *twenty28.co* for an affordable solution. In today's world, and especially in the world of tomorrow, a web presence is a non-negotiable for any church interested in anyone new ever coming through their doors.

Have Fun with One Another

Do you know what I love better than a smaller church's website? Its Facebook page! Especially if it has lots of photos from picnics and fellowships and special events. One criticism aimed at Jesus during His earthly ministry was that He liked to party—often with nonreligious people. Smaller churches do this well. Or at least they can. Fellowship is a spiritual discipline that takes planning. Adult classes could set a goal of having a party or another social activity once a month. You don't have to be legalistic about it. For example, you could skip November and have a Christmas party early in December. Or skip June, July, or September if your church has a big Vacation Bible School family night, an Independence Day celebration, or a Labor Day picnic.

Serve with One Another While You Have Fun!

Parties help a community come together in fellowship. But if you really want to see your group bond in fellowship, do a ministry project together. It could be something as simple as raking the leaves of a homebound widow or cleaning the house of a hospitalized class member. Or it could be something more costly, like preparing and serving meals at a homeless shelter. You may want to start with baby-step projects like collecting school supplies, clothing, or food for your church's benevolence ministry. In terms of developing real community, nothing beats actually doing something purposeful together.

The Moment of Truth

Let's say everything has gone well for a guest so far. They've parked close to the building and been greeted warmly. They've been accompanied to their Sunday School classroom. Someone has completed the "Baptist paperwork" for them and introduced them to the class. So far, so good. Now the moment of truth: the Bible study experience itself.

2. Expect a Great Bible Study Experience Every Week

Expect every class to have a great experience learning from the Bible every week. Every week? You can already guess our answer. Yes, every week! Great curriculum helps.

Bible Study in an Open Group Philosophy

A commitment to keeping Sunday School classes open both impacts and is impacted by the approach to Bible study. More on that later. The most important principle is this: Every individual Bible study session needs to be a complete and satisfying experience. It may—and probably should—be part of a larger unit of study that connects the lessons together. Nevertheless, for a person attending the group for the very first time, it should also be a complete experience, with ...

- *introductory comments, questions or activities,*

- *comments, questions, or activities that encourage the discovery and application of the truths of the Scripture passage or story, and*

- *a satisfying conclusion that hopefully equips members to answer or at least wrestle with the question, "So what?"*

When members know they can count on this approach, it dramatically increases the likelihood that they'll invite someone new to class. It's not just a sound educational model, it's an important element of the psychology of invitation.

What the Room Set-up Signals

Rows of chairs with a lectern at the front signals that the leader will do most of the talking and the learners will sit and listen. Some people prefer this arrangement because it is safe: nobody is looking at me, and I don't have to say anything! This is about the only way to set up a class where attendance exceeds 25 to 30. The use of smaller buzz groups during class is an effective way to stimulate participation in such a class.

A semicircle with the leader sitting or standing in the open end signals there will be some level of participation, but the leader is still clearly in charge. (This is my favorite way to teach, but it may not be the best way!)

A full circle signals that the leader is a fellow learner, and there is going to be a lot of interaction in this class. It is also the most efficient use of space because you use every wall.

Put Guests at Ease

It's scary to go to a new church, and even more so if you have never been in any church. But at least you can be somewhat anonymous in a larger crowd. So sometimes it can be even more scary to go to a small group for the first time. Do you do everything you can to make sure your group works together to create the kind of environment and experiences in your class that makes newcomers feel welcome and at ease? If that's your goal, and it should be, here are some "nevers" to help you get there:

- *Never ask a guest to fill out a form; do it for them.*

- *Never ask a newcomer to stand and introduce themselves; the person who filled out the form introduces them, sharing interesting information not included on the form!*

- *Never call on a newcomer to pray or read without making sure it's OK ahead of time.*

This last point might seem like a small thing, but one very common and real fear among many participants is that they will be called on to read out loud. Establish an atmosphere in which newcomers can attend without worrying that they will be asked to speak out loud.

Use the Personal Study Guide

Ideally, every person in the class will have a copy of the member resource during the class session. Isn't that a little old fashioned? Maybe. But it still works! It makes members feel more confident and guests feel more comfortable. A high expectations class encourages each participant to do some preparation for the session. The minimum level of preparation is reading the Scripture passage. Since the passage is printed in most LifeWay curriculum materials, guests need not be embarrassed by trying to find the passage in their Bible even if they brought one. Often, the Personal Study Guide will have discussion questions, photos, and other activities teachers can use during the session to enliven the lecture or provoke discussion. Having everything they need right in the Personal Study Guide helps create a climate that feels "safe" for a newcomer.

Providing the guest a Personal Study Guide they can have as their own also communicates that they have a place in the group and are expected to come back.

Send Activity Sheets Home

Make sure parents understand that these simple kids' pages, which typically include the Bible story and perhaps an activity, are provided to help them reinforce the Bible story at home. There is also a possible bonus effect on many moms and dads. If they do not know the Lord, they will be exposed week after week to a Bible story. The take-home sheet is one of the oldest traditions of the Sunday School movement. But it's an old idea that's still a good one!

3. Expect to Follow-up Aggressively

Two Categories of Prospects

There are basically two categories of prospective members: those who are looking and those who are lost. Unfortunately, many churches are set up to grow only by reaching out to the first group. In truth, though, a good website is all you may need for that particular group. If you want to reach the second group, you need more. Just as wise business leaders seek ways to tell a wider audience about their products or services, so do wise Sunday School leaders. Visitation is just a smart and effective way to go about "the Father's business" of offering our community what money can't buy: a life worth living forever—abundant, eternal life through Jesus Christ and His church.

Face-to-Face Contact

In a sophisticated, technological society like ours, isn't visitation a little old fashioned? Well, if American business would stop doing it, we could take care of our air traffic challenges immediately! Most of the business people you see on an airliner are "out on visitation." They could have reached out and touched that potential customer by telephone or written them a note. In fact, they probably have and will. But they know that there is absolutely no substitute for a face-to-face contact with the customer or prospective customer. So they invest in visitation.

Getting it Backward?

Many Sunday School leaders follow-up with a worship service guest by sending a letter or other written communication. If that is not successful, they make a phone call. If that doesn't work, then perhaps the Sunday School leader considers making a home visit. That's backward! If you would make a face-to-face contact early in the process, the other methods could build on that experience rather than lead up to it. Imagine that it is the first week after a guest has filled out a guest card for the first time. You and perhaps a team of one or two others make an at-the-door visit to introduce yourselves and invite the guest to your Bible study group. It's not even that important for you to get into his residence. The important thing is that you have a face-to face encounter. When you call him later in the week to reinforce your invitation, he can associate your face with your voice. After that, an e-mail or a note in the mail serves to reinforce your personal efforts. In fact, you may need no further face-to-face contacts at all, if you'll just make one early in the process.

Leave Something

Always take something to leave behind when you visit a prospective member. Leaving a Sunday School Personal Study Guide says, "We really want you to be involved in our class, and this will help you get a head start." A family magazine or devotional resource is always valued. A brochure about what the church believes and what ministries it offers is always appreciated. Some churches leave a mug, a pen, or some other "ad specialty" gift. Regardless of what you leave, always leave your name, phone number, and e-mail address!

Definite...

A successful outreach program needs ...
- *Definite prospects,*
- *Definite time to go out,*
- *Definite reporting process, and*
- *A Definite Outreach Leader as champion.*

4. Expect People to Say Yes

Don't say no for other people. Expect people to say yes! We are fans of only counting yes votes. David once answered a question about funding a new multi-purpose building. A man known for being divisive asked, "Are we voting on how we'll raise the money for this building?" My reply: "Yes, we are. Each vote costs one dollar. And you can vote as many times as you want. When we get enough yes votes, we'll start the building!"

Yes to an Invitation to Attend

In an upcoming chapter, we will talk about developing a culture of invitation, but for now, consider what a culture like that might look like. It means members regularly invite new people to attend, and they expect those people to say yes to your invitation! After all, why wouldn't they? Look at all the things you've done to get ready for company! You really expect new people every week, and it shows in dozens of ways, large and small. And when they come, the Bible study experience is a dynamic one in every class, from the preschool class to the adult class. You're ready! Now it's time to start inviting people to attend, expecting them to say yes, with great confidence that they'll say yes over and over again because of the wonderful experience they've had.

Yes to Enrollment

Open enrollment means people can belong before they believe. They don't have to believe the Bible. They don't have to be Christians. They don't even have to like God! They just have to accept an invitation to enroll as members of the class.

Yes to Preparation

It's a good and right thing to expect members to come prepared for the class session. That's one of the advantages of providing inexpensive printed curriculum materials, or at least sending a weekly e-mail and/or attachment to members so they can know what Scripture passage you will explore, main topic you will discuss, or key issues you will examine. You also may provide some commentary or questions to think about ahead of class. That kind of preparation ropes guests in, compelling them to actually come back for next week.

Along with your invitation, you can provide a copy of the study material you are using. If you are using what we call "ongoing" material at LifeWay, you can say something like this in conjunction with your invitation: "Here's a booklet with the topics and Scriptures we're studying in our class right now. Before you come, you might want to take a few minutes to find the study for that weekend in the book, and read ahead. The Scripture passage is printed right there in the book, along with an author's comments about what it means. I think you'll enjoy reading it whether you come that week or not." That doesn't sound that hard, does it? And guess what? By that simple act, you have removed the number one barrier for adults: thinking they know too little about the Bible to participate. Just don't tell them they may be better prepared than some of the regulars! But what if they never come? You've still provided them a valuable Bible study guide. If it's LifeWay material, it will usually include a plan of salvation on the inside front cover. It's an investment in eternity that costs a few cents a lesson—plus enough love to make the invitation.

Yes to Serving in the Class

The reason many teachers don't have helpers is that they don't ask. The reason they don't ask is that they don't expect members to say yes. So ask people. And expect them to say yes. There is a proper way to ask. And many improper ways! The most improper way is to stand before the class and ask for volunteers. You'll get two responses, both bad:

- *No one will respond.*

- *Someone will respond, but they're a poor fit for the job.*

What's the proper way to ask people to serve? Ask a specific person to consider a specific job for a specific period of time. Pray about it. When you sense God has confirmed a name, make an appointment to talk with that person. Never go into that conversation with a second choice. This is the person God has impressed you to ask. There is not a backup plan. Spell out the responsibilities of the job. Neither over-sell nor under-sell the expectations. Tell them you won't take an immediate answer, even if it's yes! Ask them if they'll pray about it. If they say yes, assure them that whatever God tells them to do will be OK with you. Call in a few days to get their answer. Expect a yes!

Yes to Releasing Missionaries to Kids

A chief indicator that an adult class is becoming a mature community is that it rejoices when it releases members to serve as missionaries to preschoolers, kids, and students. Many classes and small groups grow so inwardly focused that they seldom release anyone to serve with kids, much less rejoice over the fact. Healthy classes create a culture that encourages people to leave the class to serve. They assign a top care-group leader to associate members who have left to serve. Classes invite them to parties. They pray for them regularly. They treat them like what they are: missionaries to kids! They display photos of them on a wall or bulletin board, preferably candid shots from the rooms that are their mission fields. They lift them up as examples. When a class builds that kind of culture, a remarkable thing happens: people say yes to serving kids. What's so important about that? Simply this astonishing fact: the overwhelming majority of people who come to Christ as Savior and Lord will do so before his or her 18th birthday. When a class actively and joyfully releases their members to serve, it reinforces the outward focused mindset that should pervade every class that wants to grow.

Yes to Evangelistic Prayer

Another possible first step in missions involvement might be to engage your class in intentional evangelistic prayer. Put up a tear sheet or poster board on the wall and start listing the names or initials of people who don't know Jesus. Refer to it weekly as you get updates. Celebrate when you learn that someone on the list has said yes to Christ. Listen to the prayer requests. Do they increasingly concern the thing God cares most about: seeking, serving, and saving the lost? Are they voiced with great expectations that God will hear and answer those prayers and that we can be part of the answer?

Yes to New Ideas

The Sunday School movement has experienced many changes over the past 200 years. It needs to remain open to saying yes to new ideas. Think changing the name to something cooler or more contemporary will help you reach and teach more people in your community? Go for it! Think offering Bible study groups that function like Sunday School but meet on a weekday or weeknight might help you reach people who can't attend on Sundays? Do it! Would setting up a Facebook group for your class help people stay connected? Set it up! Need to utilize a large space by having table groups and a master teacher? Try it! Want to explore the possibility of a conference-call class for homebound members, an Internet chat (or Skype) class for deployed military personnel, or a Twitter #hashtag class for college students away at school? Experiment with it!

... And Maybe a Few Old Ones!

All of these ideas were once considered innovative or ingenious. Maybe we could say yes to some of them again. Let's re-explore these classic ideas.

Literature Distribution

This classic practice centered on a simple idea: take a copy of the Personal Study Guide to every person on the class ministry list before the beginning of each new quarter. Isn't that a lot to expect? Absolutely! It reinforces the personal commitment required to grow as a disciple and a church member. And a practice built on great excuses. You see, it gives a class leader a great excuse to drop by a member's home for a quick, at-the-door, "Don't want to come in" visit; say a brief word about the upcoming Bible study; and ask whether the member has any prayer needs. It helps overcome the main excuses people have for not attending Sunday School: they don't feel they're wanted, and they don't feel confident in their knowledge of the Bible. Organizationally, this practice provides a great excuse to enlist and deploy care-group leaders. Isn't that an expensive investment? If you use LifeWay materials, it's 2-3 dollars a person. Even the most penny-minded finance committee can understand you investing in the lives of people, trying to stay in regular touch with members, and providing Bible study material from their church—whether or not they attend. (I (David) am absolutely confident that such an effort more than pays for itself—in attendance and giving. But then, I sort of operate on great expectations!)

Door-to-door Visits

Since the previous idea is based on the premise that at-the-door visits are still possible in our cocooned society, let's explore that classic idea as well. I hear a lot of people including pastors say, "You can't knock on doors in our community." But you know what? I keep hearing stories from pastors who are challenging that idea with remarkable results. Maybe visitation is an old idea we ought to say yes to again!

Visitation: "We don't want to come in...."

This strategy was developed as a compromise to a twin dilemma. On the one hand, it's sort of uncomfortable—and perhaps counterproductive—to have someone show up at the door unannounced. Likely, the person's house is not ready for company. So the solution some churches employ is to make appointments. The problem with asking for appointments is that it usually doesn't work! Elmer Towns reported that the track record at Thomas Road Baptist Church was that 50 percent of the people they called to make an appointment with said, "No thanks." Of the 50 percent who said, "Sure," half of them would not be home at the time of the appointment. Thus the compromise: drop by a prospective member's house unannounced, but announce quickly at the door, "We don't want to come in!" You'll see immediate relief on the face of the person you're visiting, and you'll accomplish what you dropped by for:

- *Thanking them for visiting and inviting them back;*

- *Delivering information about the church; and*

- *Most importantly, seeing each other face-to-face.*

All without trying to get in. It's certainly a different strategy, but worth giving a try, especially if leaders don't yet feel comfortable in doing traditional visitation.

Develop Six Dynamics of a Culture of Invitation

Every environment has a culture. A home, a workplace, a locker room, a living room; each one has its own culture. The culture is the set of unwritten rules that everyone intuitively knows and abides by in a given environment. Churches and classes that want to grow develop a culture of invitation that carries an expectation of invite others.

The Psychology of Invitation

Imagine a leaky faucet. Regardless of how hard you twist the knob, it still drips. One drop at a time. The incessant drip, drip, drip. The consistency becomes an annoyance pretty quickly. But put in the right environment and given enough time, that same dripping with that same consistency can have an immense amount of power.

That's how canyons are made. Not all at once, but through the power of consistency. Dripping isn't that exciting, but what it lacks in flash it makes up for in effectiveness. There's a lot to be said for the power of consistency.

Consistency is essential to build trust in the minds and hearts of members. If your class is consistently driven by an every-week expectation that new people may be present, members will learn to trust in that consistency. The result is the removal of a significant psychological barrier that makes members less hesitant to invite new people to Bible study. That's what we call the psychology of invitation.

Anyone Is Welcome Any Week

Well, of course, new people are welcome in our class every week! Who wouldn't affirm that? That's what we call the theology of invitation. Simply stated, we know the Bible exhorts us to compel others to come and to expect new people every week, treating them with honor when they do. We have it right theologically. But sometimes we do things that pit theology against sociology. Usually, these are not intentional actions. They grow from a sort of group subconscious. You see, there is also a sociology of invitation. The natural inertia for a small group, a class, or a church is to become a closed group. It takes almost no effort to become closed.

It's the predictable course of group dynamics. It takes great effort, on the other hand, for a group to intentionally remain open.

- *Culture of invitation: A willingness for class members to invite people to Sunday School*

- *Psychology of invitation: A mind-set that class members expect new people to be present any given Sunday*

- *Theology of invitation: A conviction that God wants believers to invite others to Bible study*

- *Sociology of invitation: A group's intentional effort to remain open to newcomers*

Through consistency, we can indeed create truly open groups and an open church. Here are six dynamics that contribute to that openness.

1. Invigorate

The first step in developing a culture of invitation is to invigorate the environment and experiences in your church or class. In other words, you want to make your church, class, or group a great experience for the people who show up.

Often, this is simpler than people think. Don't think in terms of smoke, lights, or expensive aesthetic improvements. Think instead of the power of people and simple but effective tools in their hands.

For example, what is the first thing guests experience when they pull up on the church property? Do they see just another building with myriads of doors that lead to a variety of places, or do they see a smiling volunteer welcoming them and asking them if they can help them find anything?

In terms of a classroom, small and simple changes to the environment can be a great catalyst to invigorate that experience. Consider all the sights, smells, sounds, and even touches that might be pleasing to a first time guest. Simple actions like having music playing in the background when people enter the room, having a light scent in the air, or a basic welcome sign can go a long way.

But maybe the most effective thing a leader can do in this respect is to make it his goal to be the first one in the room. Always. That way the leader ensures that no guest will ever the first person to walk in and there is always someone to make guests feel welcome.

What's more, leaders can be prepared for these interactions. Every leader should have a dozen or so basic "get to know you" questions in their minds when meeting someone for the first time. Things like, "Tell me about your family," "What type of work do you do?" "Tell me about your upbringing. What did you like the most about it?" Try to make them feel at ease and avoid any awkwardness that might color the experience when someone looks back on it.

2. Incorporate

Churches and groups can learn from the retail environment. Jesus said, "I must be about my Father's business." What is the Father's business? It's the business of reaching and redeeming people. Although the church is not a business in the same sense a store is, churches can learn from retailers when it comes to reaching people and turning them into loyal customers. We are compelled to do so since our mission has eternal ramifications.

There are principles, then, that we should incorporate into our culture of invitation. Think, for example, about something like traffic. The goal of most brick and mortar retailers is to increase their store traffic, knowing that if they can just get people in the door, what they have to offer them will be attractive enough to make them spend their money. So how does a church increase its traffic? It's through outreach oriented events and initiatives. For example, churches can allow their property to be used by the community, hosting events like "trunk or treat" or a Memorial Day Picnic in order to generate that traffic.

Also an individual class can increase the foot traffic. Teachers and group leaders should care enough about their group to make their case for having the most accessible rooms and the best equipment available. Further, they should make sure to have clear signage and clear descriptions of what each class is studying. These are simple ways to get more people in the door.

Retailers also make use of another valuable commodity: names. If a retailer can gain access to the names, addresses, or email addresses of potential customers, then they are going to talk to them in a variety of ways. So also should the church and the group.

No one should be anonymous and all information should be acted upon. A church and a class should have an intentional and non-confrontational strategy to following up personally with every guest, learning more and more about them, so they can know how to minister to them. This begins as soon as someone walks in the door and is presented, along with regular attenders and members, with a nametag so they can be called by name. And later in the week, they should receive some kind of personal communication thanking them for visiting, making sure to answer all their questions, and inviting them to come back. A face-to-face visit is usually better than a call, text, or e-mail.

Another practice the church can use is to advertise and inform. Retailers make sure potential customers know what's coming, whether a sale or a special promotion. The church must also be forward thinking in this respect. A teacher or group leader should be able to clearly describe to their people the next topic of study and how to prepare for it. Doing so piques interest and is another chance to invite people back again and again. It also helps people know that, even if they don't resonate with a particular topic, a new one will come along soon enough.

3. Intercede

Intercession is the key to developing a culture of invitation. Something remarkable happens when church people start praying for their church, pastor, class, teacher, and other church members. If a class or group is struggling to reach outside themselves, then prayer is a great first step.

Through prayer, the Lord not only answers the request, but He molds our hearts to deeply feel the request. Even if a class doesn't really want new people to join, they can begin praying for it to happen, and then slowly but surely the Holy Spirit will begin to align the hearts of those who pray with the prayers they are praying.

For the class, this can take a variety of different forms, but it must be an intentional effort on the part of the leader. Without shaming anyone for offering personal prayer requests, the leader can begin to shift the conversation away from "me" and onto "them." For example, a leader might commit that every week the class is going to have a 5-minute prayer focus for some area of the community. They might bring pictures of a specific subdivision, apartment complex, or trailer park. They could even dig into the census data of their community to give a realistic picture of the environment where the Lord has placed them for ministry. The key is the specific nature of those prayers.

As long as we are praying for a general "them," we will find our hearts slow in coming alongside that prayer. But when we can give names, faces, and even statistics to that "them," people will genuinely begin to feel the urgency of the request. And they will put action to the prayers.

4. Invest

Because Christ Himself is in the business of meeting needs, His church is also in the business of meeting needs. Through His ministry, Jesus' life was characterized by His investment in the lives of others, meeting their needs and challenging them to something higher and greater than themselves, inviting His followers to invest their lives in the grand agenda of the kingdom of God.

Too many churches start their long range planning discussions with the wrong question: How can we get more people to come to our church? An investment question would be better: What unmet needs exist in our community and how might we invest some of our resources to meet one or more of those needs?

This doesn't have to be an expensive endeavor. Distribute cold water at a parade with labels that include the church's name and worship times. Wash car windows in a parking lot and leave a little note. Offer after school tutoring with church members as volunteer teachers. The list goes on and on.

For the individual class or group, class projects can be great investments, too. Clean up a park. Adopt the faculty of an elementary school and bring an occasional meal or snack to them. Send a group to help folks in an assisted living facility worship and study the Bible on Sundays. Mow yards, paint fences, or clean gutters. The point for all these things is that it not only forces the group into a rhythm of thinking outside themselves, but it also makes that church or group very attractive to those on the outside.

Sometimes that means the people who are ministered to, but in a larger sense, it's a wonderful message to a community about the church or group's willingness to see needs and meet them.

5. Invite

You've seen by now there is a lot more to creating a culture of invitation in your church or class than just inviting others. That being said, most people still won't come unless someone personally invites them.

In other words, think of the invitation as reaping the fruit many of the above actions helped to plant, grow, and water. For example, an invitation might come to a man who saw a sign, then had his windows washed, and then finally had a coworker mention his group to him. That invitation struck a chord that had been created by all the other actions the church or group had taken.

Statistics tell us that people are more receptive to an invitation on certain occasions, such as moving to a new community, a marriage, the birth of a child, or some loss in their lives. Furthermore, if a group or church is in the rhythm of providing occasions when it's easy to bring a guest, like group fellowships or church-wide community events, then the invitation becomes even easier.

But you know what all these things have in common? They're all kingdom perspectives that come when a class, a group, or a church actively looks for opportunities in their daily relationships.

When you have a culture of invitation in the church, members are on the hunt. They are actively engaging in building relationships for the sake of the gospel. They know if they can get that person in the door, they will have a great and potentially life-changing experience.

Of course, this kind of invitation paves the way for the greater invitation to come. This is the invitation that Jesus makes with open arms; that "whosoever will" might find forgiveness for their sins and be saved.

6. Involve

Bringing together everyone and pooling their gifts, passions, experiences, and backgrounds is absolutely essential for a church or class that is serious about developing a culture of innovation. It's a team effort. But in order to make that happen, every person must begin to see himself or herself as an essential part of the process God uses to bring people to Himself.

How do we get there? The first step is through knowledge. Both a leader and an individual member must have knowledge of each person's spiritual gifts. Based on that knowledge, the leader must work not to just fill a need, but to create opportunity for each member to serve within his giftedness.

Think about the example of outreach. Some group members might be gifted in evangelism, but others might be better at writing cards or providing childcare for those doing visits to homes.

Or think about the class in general. We typically think of serving in a group exclusively in terms of teaching, but what about utilizing the gift of helps to create a calendar for providing meals for those who are sick? What about using the gift of administration to make a concerted effort at group retention? What if a person with the gift of compassion maintained a weekly prayer list to be distributed to all involved in the group?

All of these provide the kind of teamwork a culture of invitation needs. What's more, when people observe the roles that others play, they begin to see their involvement in the group not as something optional, but as something they must do in order to play the part only they can fulfill.

Act on Five Proven Steps to Growth

K-E-E-P. GO! This acrostic is a way to remember a 5-stage formula that has helped Sunday Schools grow since Arthur Flake proposed it in 1920.[6] We have added some "D" words to update it a bit.

A Slight Twist on a 100 Year-old Formula that Still Works		
Flake's Formula	Francis' Flaky Formula	
Know the possibilities	Dream	Imagine what could be; where it could be; how it might be.
Enlarge the organization	Declare	Announce the groups you'll launch before you need them or have the leaders for them.
Enlist and train the leaders	Develop	Call out and develop leaders who can develop leaders.
Provide space & resources	Determine	Plan wisely to feed people in places conducive to Biblical community.
GO after the people!	Deploy	Launch new groups that will not wait to be found but will go find people.

1. Dream: Imagine the Possibilities

Is it within the scope of reason that your church could reach 100 in Sunday School attendance? 125? 150?

Accurately Assess Current Reality

The first task of vision casting or goal setting is an accurate assessment of the current reality. Have a conversation about these issues as you consider a path past 100.

Primary Ministry Area (PMA)

What is your PMA? That is, what is the primary geographical area you believe God has assigned to your church? Can you draw your PMA on a map or describe it in some other way? What natural, political, psychological, sociological, or transportation boundaries best define your PMA? How many live in your PMA? Is it possible that 100 of them might attend Sunday School at your church? More? What needs exist in the PMA that your church might tackle?

Momentum

Churches that average less than 100 fall into three broad categories in terms of momentum:

- *A new church that is growing but not yet to 100.*
- *An old church that once averaged more than 100, but has declined.*
- *A church that started small, stayed small, and is still small.*

Each of these has its unique challenges. What do you think might be the challenges of each? The advantages? Which one best describes your church? Do those challenges and advantages apply to you?

2. Declare: Enlarge the Organization

The main idea here is to decide to add new classes in anticipation of growth rather than only in response to it. Most of us are better at dreaming than implementing! I believe there is an important interim step between dreaming and doing—a declaration phase. That is even easier if you are just setting up a table and putting a sign on it.

3. Develop: Enlist and Train the Leaders

You can't just declare leaders. They must be enlisted and developed. Don't say "no" for anyone. Even busy people deserve to discover the deep satisfaction that comes from doing Sunday School work. Don't appeal publicly for volunteers. The main reason many people do not volunteer is because they have never been asked personally in a prayerful, compelling way. Pray. Ask God to impress a name upon you. Meet. A phone call, e-mail, text message, or chance meeting won't do. Sit down with the person. Enlist to a vision more than to a set of tasks. Maybe share a book like this one. Don't accept an answer at the initial meeting. Ask the person to pray. I like to simply ask, "Will you pray about it?" Usually they answer yes to that. I respond, "Me, too. And whatever God tells you to do will be okay with me." And it must be! Then in a few days, call to ask the person for an answer. If they say no, start over. Never have a "number two." If asked, respond, "I don't know. I will start the process over again." If they say yes, provide training. The best training is done on the job.

Perhaps the most effective way to learn a Sunday School position is to serve along with someone who is already experienced. Teachers can enlist a promising apprentice, with the goal of seeing them start a new class at the appropriate time. My wife Vickie and I teach a Preschool Sunday School class. Chris and Dana served with us for several months before taking a class themselves and testify to the effectiveness of this method.

4. Determine: Plan for Providing Space and Resources

Even if you've declared a new class and enlisted a new leader, you still must provide a place, furnishings, equipment, and study materials.

The Curriculum Connection

The choice of curriculum is important not only for ongoing Bible study but also in the enlistment and training of teachers and leaders. We do not want a person who is sitting in an adult class observing the teacher to think "I could never do that." Rather, we want them to think, "I could do that if they gave me the same resources." The trend toward allowing adult teachers to "do their own thing" is reversing. Today many growing churches are asking their adult teachers to use the same curriculum or limiting their choices of curriculum. It is incredibly more efficient to enlist and train new leaders if all leaders are using similar curriculum. It is easier to supply support materials. It is easier to enlist and equip substitutes—who are potential future apprentices.

5. Deploy: GO after the People

Deploy implies action. Classes must not wait for people to find them. We must deploy to invite people. And be deliberate about it. In a passive approach, worship attenders are told, "Getting into a Sunday School class is important. You need to find one." Another scenario illustrates a deliberate approach. Worship participants are told, "Getting into a Sunday School class is important. We will help you find one. In fact, we believe that it is so important, you can expect a class to come find you!" New classes do that best.

Embrace Four Foundational Principles

There are at least four principles your church should embrace if you want to grow past the 100 barrier.

1. Care for Every Person

One of the things that sets apart a healthy Sunday School from a struggling one is a commitment to care for every person. Nothing says "we care" like a Sunday School with a vital and functioning system of care groups. Ideally, this means that every person is assigned to a care group and that every care group has a leader. The mission of the care group and the job description of the care group leader are the same:

Contact Every Member Every Week

Do you mean every absent member every week? Nope. I mean every member every week. The contact can be face-to-face, by phone, or by e-mail. Or on a really special occasion, like a birthday or an anniversary, the care group leader might make the special effort of mailing a card. The responsibility of the care-group leader is not to get people to come to class. The role of the care-group leader is to help members connect in community. In fact, care group leaders should seldom mention class attendance. Rather, their role is:

- *"Just keeping in touch."*
- *"Just checking in to see how you're doing."*
- *"Anything going on you'd like the class to pray about?"*

The contacts need not be long. Just a quick phone call during a daily commute will do. The goal is simply to stay connected with every person in the group and to report news and needs to the teacher and, in urgent cases, to the pastor so that the appropriate person can make a timely ministry response. Many people, properly enlisted, will be ready to accept this entry-level leadership position—one that's very important yet not overwhelming.

5-7 Men or Women

Best practice suggests that each adult care group leader will assume responsibility for five to seven men or women. Men should contact men and women should contact women. Why not have couples' care groups? Because usually the women will contact the women but the men won't. Besides you don't want to place people in potential positions that could lead to a compromise. Not surprisingly, this sets up a perfect organization to communicate information related to women's or men's ministries, too, without creating a separate organization!

Every Person Assigned

Each member should be assigned to a care group. Some classes call these ministry groups. You might even call them connect groups. I have also heard the groups called CPR groups to signify the three purposes of the group: care, prayer, and reaching. It matters less what you call them than that you do them! Groups should start with about five members, with a maximum of seven. Starting with fewer allows you to add new members. Seven is a good maximum because there are seven days in a week, which means a group leader could contact one member each day. Once several group leaders have seven members, enlist new group leaders so you can get group numbers back down to five.

Care Groups on Steroids

The previous paragraph describes a relatively passive care group. Nobody except the care group leader might even know who is in the group. That's OK. It's a start. And it's certainly preferable to not having care groups at all. But care groups can be and do more, especially if your class is intentional about becoming a community. One step forward is to reserve 10 to 15 minutes at the beginning or end of every class session for the class to gather into care groups. Some classes even check attendance in these groups. During this time the group has two primary objectives:

- *Calling the names of all absent group members to identify ministry needs*
- *Sharing and praying with one another*

This is one of the primary reasons for having single-gender care groups. Women and men often have different kinds of prayer needs and are usually more likely to share them if the group includes only their gender.

2. Open Groups

Here is a short definition we have found useful:

An open group expects new people every week.

The practice of open groups is the foundational principle of a growing Sunday School. If you really do expect new people every week, that expectation will drive everything else you do before, during, and after a newcomer experiences it. Everything! Leaders arrive early. The room is set up with newcomers in mind. Every lesson is a complete and satisfying Bible study experience. All this goes against the grain. The natural inertia of any group is to become closed. It takes vigilance to remain open. To be a welcoming place for newcomers every week. To be an easy next step for someone when they decide to move beyond worship attendance alone. Do you expect new people every week? How would we know?

An open group is an intentional mix of believers and unbelievers, saved and unsaved, churched and unchurched, biblical scholars and biblical novices. How intentional that mix is depends on you. And it will take effort to keep your group open, especially if it has been together for more than a couple of years. Because Sunday School classes are open groups, choose curriculum materials that support keeping them open. Each Bible study experience should be self-contained. That is the primary advantage of ongoing curriculum resources. They allow learners to engage in a unit of study around a topic, character, or book of the Bible, but each lesson also stands on its own. Every lesson provides a satisfying experience for the first-time guest, the long-time absentee, the every-other-week attender, and the never-misses-a-Sunday member.

The Empty Chair

The symbol of an open group is the empty chair. Lyman Coleman popularized this concept.[7] The idea is to always have an empty chair (or two if a couples class). What if the room is packed full? Find a way to have an extra chair! Any empty chair is a reminder that the class is not just about us! The chair also sparks conversation about who could be sitting in that chair: absentees, inactive members, prospects, church members not yet connected to a small group. How many empty chairs do you need?

3. Open Enrollment

Sunday School classes are designed to be open groups that practice open enrollment. Open enrollment means you can:

Belong before you believe.

Enrolling as a member of a Sunday School class is a great first step for people who have not yet decided whether they want to join the church, pledged allegiance to Jesus as Savior and Lord, or identified with Christ publicly through baptism, or while exploring Christianity and the Bible. They need to understand that enrolling in Sunday School does not make them a church member or a Christian. Nor obligate them to become one. It's just a way to belong before they believe. Whether they ever do or not.

Ministry List

You do not ask someone to enroll as an expression of their commitment to the class. We ask people to enroll as a way of expressing the class's commitment to them. That's why it may be better to think of the "roll" more as a "ministry list." It is a list of members who have made a covenant to pray for one another and care for one another. Do you regularly invite people to enroll? Or better, "May we add you to our ministry list?"

Church Membership Not Required

What if, when asked about enrolling as a member of your group, someone says, "We're not sure we're ready to join the church"? I recommend that you memorize this response: "Enrolling as a member of our class does not make you a member of the church, nor does it obligate you to become one." Communicating both points is important. We want Sunday School members to understand that enrolling in the class, making a commitment to Christ, and requesting church membership are three distinct and separate decisions. And we also want them to know that a lot of people enroll as members of Sunday School while they are considering one or more of those decisions. It's sort of like trial membership in the church.

You may be amazed how many people will respond positively to such an invitation if presented in a clear, compelling way. Beyond the mechanics of enrollment, however, what people are really listening for is "We like you;

we want to get to know you better; would you honor us by being an official member of our group?" They want to know it's OK with you if they belong before they believe—even if they never believe.

Enrollment and Assimilation

Assimilation is a word used by church leaders to describe the process and the problem of connecting to a local church after accepting Jesus' offer of forgiveness and eternal life. The problem primarily arises from an approach to evangelism that suggests this process: conversation, conversion, community. This approach suggests that the normal way to reach people for Christ is to present the gospel to them, lead them to pray to receive Christ, then try to help them connect with a group or church where they can grow in Christ. Thus, the problem of assimilation is accomplishing the third step in that process. And it is a real problem because, unfortunately, it is quite rare when this approach actually results in the person's getting to the third step—being assimilated into a local church.

Dozens of schemes have been devised to solve this problem, but most have had disappointing results. So what if we changed the order of the process? What if our primary process were conversation, community, conversion? That is, the goal of conversations with our friends, relatives, associates, acquaintances, and neighbors would be to invite them to be part of our Bible study group; then to invite them to enroll in the class and become part of our community; and finally, in the context of fellowship around God's Word, experience Christ's love and their need for Him. When a person comes to Christ this way, guess what happens to the problem of assimilation? There's not one! They are already assimilated! Enrollment and participation in a Sunday School class or small group is perhaps the grandest pre-assimilation tool ever!

Anytime; Anywhere

Leaders and members alike can invite any person—indeed, every newcomer—to enroll at any time. Will people enroll in Sunday School? Yes! But leaders and members must invite them to enroll! I have found it remarkably easy to enroll new members over the telephone. For many years as a minister of education, my goal was to enroll at least one person in Sunday School before leaving the office on Wednesday evening. The conversation usually went something like this:

"Hi, Jim, this is David Francis from First Baptist Church. I've seen you and your family visiting our Bible study, and wanted to know if you would like to be enrolled in Sunday School?" Typically, they would respond with something like "We're not really ready to make a commitment to the church yet." I would reply, "You don't have to make a commitment to church membership to become a member of the Sunday School. We have a lot of people who attend our church who enroll as Sunday School members while they are considering whether to become church members or Christians. If you choose to enroll in a Bible study group, you'll enjoy most of the benefits of church membership. We'll put you on the regular mailing list to receive our church newsletter. We'll even send you offering envelopes! About the only things you can't do is hold a leadership position or vote in business meetings. And the best thing is that you won't have to fill out any more guest forms!"

After some brief laughter, almost everyone agreed to enroll. When they asked what they needed to do, I assured them they didn't need to do anything. When they came Sunday morning, they and their children would be members of the Sunday School class they were attending. People want to belong. Invite them to enroll!

Enrollment Impacts Attendance

Nationally, Sunday School attendance averages about 50 percent of enrollment. Historically, there is an almost inexplicable correlation between enrollment and attendance. If enrollment grows, attendance goes up. If enrollment drops, attendance declines.

Enrollment Impacts Baptisms

Andy Anderson was a pastor in Florida who reached and discipled hundreds of new believers through Sunday School.[8] He is credited as being the developer of "The Sunday School Growth Spiral." Andy discovered that one out of every three lost people who were enrolled in Sunday School would accept Christ within a year. It makes sense. The more lost people we enroll in Sunday School, the more likely we are to see people come to faith in Christ. For many churches, Sunday School is not evangelistic. It can't be: no lost people are in the classes! This should be a spiritual burden, a prayer concern, a call to action. Since evangelism should be a priority of a Sunday School, enrolling lost people must also be a priority. Lost people will not study the Word if they are not present. It begins with enrolling them, mixed with accepting them, loving them, and praying for them. Enrollment:

- *Makes it more likely people will experience a sense of belonging.*
- *Establishes the context for biblical community.*
- *Makes people more likely to attend.*
- *Encourages active participation in the Bible study group.*
- *Invites the beginning of relationships.*
- *Initiates the caring ministry and regular contact.*
- *Reminds the leader of his or her role as shepherd to all.*

Open groups expect new people every week. Open enrollment makes it easy for those new people to become an official part of the group. And belong before they believe. When that happens, we need to make sure we do everything possible not to let any of these precious souls to "fall through the cracks." That is many times less likely to happen if everyone is assigned to a care group. The third foundational principle of Sunday School is that everyone is cared for.

4. The Irreducible Law of Kingdom Growth

Ideas abound about how a Sunday School, a church, or the larger kingdom of God grows. All can be reduced to this most basic principle ...

Start New Groups

On the mission field, this law means starting new preaching points, new missions, and new churches. In established churches, it means starting new groups for discipleship, ministry, and evangelism. For Sunday School, it means starting new classes. It takes incredibly vibrant leadership to persuade and equip classes to reproduce. Before we move on, we need to identify a couple of barriers to overcome if you want to start new groups.

"Our Room"

Unfortunately, the greatest obstacle to providing adequate space for expanding ministry to kids is adults who establish an ownership claim or emotional attachment to "their room." One of the sweetest sounds a Sunday School director can hear is when an adult teacher says, "Our class is willing to do whatever it takes to help us reach more people. I'll lead my class to be OK with whatever space we are assigned."

That's exactly what Ann Gregory said to me, as her class of 70-plus women moved to make room for a new preschool class. The pastor had already given up his office for the bed babies and moved into a trailer. Those are the kinds of legendary stories you can break barriers with!

The Unintentional Blocker

The number one blocker to developing an apprentice teacher and thus reproducing adult classes is the associate or team teacher who likes to teach but has no desire to ever shepherd his or her own class. What seems like a good idea results in the unintended consequence of effectively preventing a class from reproducing by blocking the number one factor in starting a new one: the apprentice teacher. The best way to deal with this obstacle is to not let it happen in the first place!

How Do We Know if It's Time to Reproduce?

There are several indicators that your class may be ready. One is that the growth of the class has plateaued. You may experience high attendance days when attendance temporarily swells, but on average the class has a fairly predictable attendance. Another clear indication is that the room is full. In fact, when it is usually 80 percent full, you should consider it full. Another indicator is that your class lacks energy.

An Apprentice

The key to successfully planting a new class is an apprentice teacher. The first step in the process is to prayerfully identify a potential apprentice. How do you do that? Just ask someone with potential to teach in your place when you're going to be out of town. When you return, casually get feedback from class members: "How did Hal do Sunday?" If the response is something like "He was OK, but we're glad you're back," you probably need to keep looking. Next time you may ask Sam to teach. If you get similar feedback, keep looking. But soon you'll get this kind of feedback: "Bob was surprisingly good! When are you going to be out of town again?" You've found your candidate! The next step is to sit down with the potential apprentice and ask him or her to pray about what you have in mind: a process of several months during which he or she will teach every time you're gone, then sometimes when you're present so that you can be a coach. Clearly state that the endgame of the process is to start a new class, with him or her as the teacher, or with you moving on to start the new group. Remember, it may be best for you to be the one who starts the new class since you are experienced, and allegiance to the current class for some members is based on you. Ask the candidate to pray about it. Covenant to keep the plan between yourselves until it's time to tell the class.

Another huge step for an on-mission class is to be intentional about reproducing itself. Are you talking about splitting our class? Not at all. That's something that gets done to you. I want to challenge you to become intentional about doing it to yourself!

The Curriculum Connection

A church or a class that adopts a curriculum plan tremendously increases the chances of successfully planting new classes. How's that work? Compare two different responses by the teacher when the apprentice asks what to teach on the Sunday he or she is out.

- *"Well, I just ask the Lord to speak to me and direct me to a passage I think the class would be interested in. Then I study my vast collection of commentaries and other resources to put the lesson together."*

- *"Here's a copy of the Leader Guide that goes with the Personal Study Guide the class is using. Just do what it says. Later you'll learn to be more creative and use other resources. But this is a good place to start."*

The advantage of using curriculum is doubly true for apprentices in preschool and children's classes, in which the use of creative activities and learning centers that relate to the Bible story are essential to a life-stage-appropriate learning experience. Maybe one of those classic ideas churches might consider saying yes to again is using quality curriculum materials!

Breaking the News

You can expect many members to resist or object to the news at first. This is how it usually goes. The teacher announces, "God has really blessed us, and I think the time has come for us to plant a new class." Lips draw in. Arms cross. Eyes glare. Obvious tension fills the room. The teacher continues, "Here's the good news! No one will be forced to take part in the new class. Everyone who wants to remain in this class can do so." No coercion. No guilt trips. People start to relax a little as you deal with their number one objection. So you continue, "But we will need a few missionaries to help start the new class. Not everybody! Just a few of you who will agree to be a core group for the new class during its infancy. We may need some of the missionaries to accept responsibility as care group leaders or other positions." The faces of a few begin to show anticipation. Then you announce that Bob will become the teacher of the new class or of the current class if you are starting the class.

At least three groups will volunteer to help start the new class:
- *Those who want the adventure of being missionaries*
- *Those who like Bob's or your teaching style*
- *A few who are experiencing relational discomfort in the class and need a gracious way to leave*

Then you announce the date. The Sunday before Easter is an excellent time, as is the beginning of a new church year. Be strategic, thinking about natural times when people may be open to something new.

Celebrating the New Plant

You cultivate what you celebrate, so when the big day comes for a new group to begin (or even better, the weekend before) make a huge deal of it. I have heard of pastors and Sunday School directors who dress in gardening clothes for a big announcement in the worship service. Both teachers are called to the front. The class may also be called forward and asked to gather around the teacher whose class is planting a new one. Then the members who have agreed to be missionaries to seed the new class gather around the new teacher. The groups don't have to be evenly divided. In fact, an appropriate goal is probably for one-third to start the new class. It may actually grow faster that way. The result is that both classes have an opportunity to experience a period of new growth at least for a couple of years.

Starting a Family Tree

Once you've determined to start birthing new classes every few years, start bragging about it! People brag about their kids and grandkids. So brag about your class' "kids"! If you've just given birth to your first class, you might want to make a poster or a wall presentation that shows your class at the top. Maybe a photo of the class. You might want to use another classic idea and have a "class photo day" as a mini-high-attendance campaign. (For added emphasis, do this on the day you're planning to announce about the new class! The crowd in of the class may amply demonstrate the need for a new one.) Then, on its first Sunday, take another photo of your "baby" class! Put it below the photo of your class, connected by a line of yarn or something. (Enlist a creative school teacher or librarian to make it look good!)

A 10-Year Plan

Now project this family tree out ten years. What will it look like then? How many new classes will your class have birthed? Two more? Three more? Does your class have any "grandkid" classes? Then brag about them, too! Ask your "daughter" class for a copy of the photo of their "daughter" they put up on their family tree!

An Experiment: Put all 4 Together

What if you could accomplish all four foundational principles at one time? As a reminder, the four principles are:
- *Caring ministry: Every member contacted every week.*
- *Open groups: Expect new people every week.*
- *Open enrollment: Belong before you believe.*
- *Irreducible law of kingdom growth: Start new groups.*

This experiment requires one big room set up with round tables or chairs arranged in horseshoes (groups of 6 or more chairs in small semi-circles, with the open end facing the focal wall). Each small group has a group leader, who serves as a care group leader and a discussion leader. Every group is open, with a couple of empty chairs. Every group has a description, so newcomers can find a group that fits them. Newcomers are encouraged to enroll right away. The care group leader begins to make weekly contacts immediately. When you are ready to start a new group, you just set up a new circle of chairs. The flow of the sessions goes something like this: the teacher gives a lecturette, then the group discusses. Another brief lecture. Group discussion. Lecture. Discussion. Then the care group leader leads the group in a time (perhaps 10 minutes) of sharing and praying. A curriculum is chosen that makes it painless for a new leader with a new group to be successful from the very first gathering. This approach can work with adults. Or students (youth). Or even both in the same room. By itself, this approach could take a church past 100 in attendance.

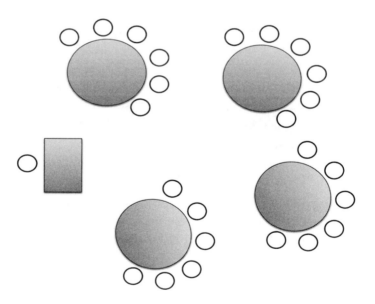

Divide the Work Around Four Age Groups

Coaches

The pastor is the head coach of the Sunday School. Every Sunday School needs four assistant coaches, each taking responsibility for one of the age-groups: Preschoolers, Kids, Students, and Adults.

Each coach is probably a player-coach. That is, he may need to enlist himself to be a teacher, a care group leader, or both. The four "divisions" follow one big idea each.

1. Preschool: Take One Baby Step

I am convinced that enlarging the preschool area is the key to growth in most churches. Yet many churches continue to hope they will grow while ignoring this key. A place to start for most churches is with babies. If you don't have a class for babies, start one. "But," you protest, "we don't have any babies." Your Sunday School will never have babies unless you provide for babies. If a couple attended your church and had no place for their newborn, it's highly unlikely they'd come back. You can't wait to respond; you must anticipate. Find a room suitable for babies. Get it sparkling clean. Paint it. Enhance the lighting. Get some safe beds and a couple of rocking chairs. Install a sink if you can. Buy some disposable gloves. Invest in smocks and enlist folks to wear them. Provide Bible study resources designed for babies. Then ask God to send you some babies. Or act like a missionary and go to the baby food aisle and interact with new parents!

2. Kids: Men Needed

With elementary children, kids simply go to the class that corresponds to their grade level without regard to how old they are or when their birthday is. That works well just about anywhere. Some churches are using a single gender approach with children. One of the key obstacles to doing this successfully is that boys need men to teach them in that environment.

Boys and girls need to see men in these key leadership roles as well as women … but not instead of women! The advance of the missionary movement known as Sunday School would have never happened without women—in reality, mostly women. I'm confident they would be happy to have some help from the guys.

3. Students: Noise Okay

Perhaps the most flexible group in your church are students. Noise doesn't bother them. As churches convert space for use by preschoolers and children, often the student area gets squeezed. If you can break the mind-set that every Sunday School class must have its own room, you can make progress with students. A solution many churches have found successful is a large room with tables as described before (see pages 49-50). Starting a new group may not require finding a new room but only setting up a new table and staffing the table with a new leader.

4. Adult: No Room Required

Could you pray for a leader to help you start one of the classes below?
- *College*
- *Nearly-weds and newlyweds*
- *Young adults (18 to 35, single or married, without kids; they don't mind being together)*
- *DINK class (dual income, no kids; you probably don't want to call it that!)*
- *Class for new parents*
- *Parents-of-teens*
- *Empty nesters*
- *Couples-without-kids class*
- *Senior adult class (believe it or not, this is a new area of ministry for many new young, contemporary churches)*

Remember, you could start a "class" in a big room by just setting up a table and enlisting a group leader. If you only needed a table, what other classes might you be able to start?

Balance Three Dimensions

In the chart below, you'll see a variety of ways leaders talk about the three priorities of a ministry of groups like Sunday School.

Dimensions of a Balanced Sunday School			
LifeWay Groups Ministry (Michael Kelley)	Disciple Making	Community Building	Culture Impacting
Transformational Groups (Stetzer & Geiger)	Formation	Connection	Mission
A Different Kind of Tribe (Rick Howerton)	Theological	Familial	Missional
		Restorational	
Simple Small Groups (Bill Search)	Changing	Connecting	Cultivating
Allan Taylor et al	Teach	Minister	Reach
David Francis — 3D Sunday School	Discover	Connect	Invite
David Francis — Discover Triad	Scripture	Shepherding	Stories
David Francis — 3 Roles	Teacher	Shepherd	Leader
David Francis — Connect3	Class	Community	Commission

Let's talk briefly about each column in this chart.

1. Disciple Making

This is the first and highest priority of any group in the church. Call it a Sunday School class, a small group, a missional community, or some clever acronym—the mission is the same: Make disciples. If any other priority trumps this as an ultimate goal, then we are failing to see what makes groups of Christians distinct from any other kind of group.

You might, for example, have a group of people that all like pizza and movies, or have kids the same age. While an affinity they might have in common might be one of the catalysts for gathering a specific group together, once gathered they must be committed to helping each other follow Jesus at a deeper level. If they are primarily committed to anything other than this goal, then you can call it a club, a frat, or a get-together; just don't call it a biblical small group.

Jesus laid out this charge clearly enough for us in Matthew 28. The resurrected Christ, instructing His disciples, first made it clear that all authority had been given to Him, whether in heaven and on earth. So what would He do with that authority?

He would command us to make disciples of all nations. The writer of Hebrews built on this command to go and make disciples in Hebrews 10:24-25: "And let us be concerned about one another in order to promote love and good works, not staying away from our worship meetings, as some habitually do, but encouraging each other, and all the more as you see the day drawing near." We should keep meeting together, but not just because we like being together. We should keep meeting together to encourage each other toward love and good works. This is discipleship.

This priority has many implications, but maybe most basic is this: We must care deeply about the centerpiece of group life. We must gather around God's Word, which reveals to us the will of God for our lives and what it means to follow Jesus as His disciples.

2. Community Building

Under the banner of making disciples, we must also prioritize community building. When we do so, we acknowledge that God does not intend for us to grow in isolation. He planned for us to help each other follow Jesus.

God Himself is a great theological basis for this priority. From the very beginning, God looked at man and said clearly that it was not good for man to be alone (Genesis 2:18). That's not because man is an inherently lonely creature; it's because we were created in God's image. And God, in His very nature, is relational. From before time began, God existed in a perfect relational harmony with Himself, perfectly content and happy as Father, Son, and Holy Spirit. Man, as the image-bearer of God, has a relational capacity and need that points us to God's own nature.

But then came sin. The fall. Everything was flipped upside down. Oh, we are still the image-bearers of God, but that image is marred and corrupted in every way imaginable including relationally. We no longer look at relationships as mutually edifying with a balance of giving and receiving built on contentment found in God alone. Now, we see people as tools to be used for our own enjoyment, gratification, or insecurity.

But God, through the gospel, redeems all things, and that includes the way we relate to one another. Indeed, we now, as the children of God, have a responsibility for one another, not just to hang out, but to make sure that we are moving together toward Christlikeness.

In short, we are friends so we can be more like Jesus. When we build community through mutual transparency, prayer for one another, and yes, even casual friendships, we are living out the image of God inside us and ultimately moving each other toward greater discipleship.

3. Culture Impacting

All groups must be disciple-making and community-building. But they must also be culture-impacting. That means that the influence of a group must extend beyond the group itself into the families, workplaces, and relationships represented within that group.

In the Sermon on the Mount, Jesus emphasized being salt and light. Just as salt and light are meant for a purpose outside themselves, groups in a church must continually make an impact on their surroundings.

Practically speaking, this means that the group must not be content with its own membership; instead, there should always be room for one more, even if that means starting another group. The groups should actively work to share the gospel, do practical service projects, and reach out in other ways with the message of the kingdom.

These three priorities should be the undergirding of what it means to be in a group. Think of these things like the skeleton in a human body. Even though we all look different at the skin level, peel away the external and we are all pretty much the same on the inside. Similarly, one church's groups might look different than another's, but at the core, the skeleton is the same. It's built on discipleship, community, and outreach.

Take it to the Next Level

Sunday School classes and small groups typically progress through three levels. Or get stuck! It's important to note that the progression here does not mean that a group moves beyond the first level; those characteristics will still be in place. But as a group matures and grows, they are able together to build on the initial level into the second and third. They move from a self-centered focus into an others-centered focus while retaining that initial basis that brought them together to begin with. Here's a chart that summarizes what those levels might look like.

	CLASS	COMMUNITY	COMMISSION
Participants	Members	Ministers	Missionaries
Focus	Me	Us	Them
Biblical Mandate	Great Confession	Great Commandment	Great Commission
"K" Words	Kerygma	Koinonia	Kenosis
Evangelism	Be nice	Be attractive	Be intentional
Conversations	What I learned	What group did for me	What we did for others
Prayer requests	General	Each other	People far from God

Let's have a quick conversation about each indicator. We'll work from left to right. As we look at these steps, we need to keep in mind that groups will move through these progressions as well as members. Just because the majority of a group may be missionaries, that doesn't mean all the members are at that level. You could also have mostly members with one or two functioning as ministers or missionaries.

Participants

Every group is made up of the participants of the group. Initially, all those participants are simply members of that group. Though it seems simple, let's not skip past that basic truth, because a "member" is someone who belongs. At this stage in group life, each person there must be committed enough, and feel the commitment enough from others, to truly own their membership. But it can't stop there.

Membership progresses to ministry. This is the moment when group members wake up to the realization that they are not only in the group to receive; they are also there to give. They begin to take on specific roles of leadership as assigned to them, but in a more organic sense, they begin to take initiative on their own to do practical things like provide meals for the sick in their group, meet up for lunch and prayer, and call and text about specific situations they know are happening in each other's lives.

Oftentimes, the group stalls out at this point. You now have a group of people who are extremely comfortable and happy with each other, and whether they know it or not, they can actually resist anyone else entering into the group for fear of disrupting the flow of life they have established together. But a strong leader of a group recognizes this tendency and actively battles against it in order to take the members who are now ministers and turn them into missionaries. They constantly push the group outward to invite, welcome, and include new people into their midst.

Biblical Mandate

The same pattern seen in the participants can also be seen in terms of what they view the Bible is calling them to do. The most basic part of any Christian's life, and therefore the initial phase of group life, is the Great Confession. That is, that Jesus is the Christ, the Son of the Living God. Until we are clear on this together, anything else we build on will be comparatively sinking sand.

But once we truly know and believe the gospel, the group must press on into the obedience of discipleship that the gospel compels. In its most simple terms, the group must help each other multiple ways everyday to flesh out what it means to love God with their heart, soul, mind, and strength, and love their neighbors as themselves. They do this not only as they study the Bible together, but as they share their own struggles, challenges, and triumphs. But it's important to note that this sharing is not only for the purpose of knowing each other better, but so that we truly can help each other move forward in specific obedience in those specific circumstances.

The movement goes from Great Confession to Great Commandment and then to Great Commission. Just as participants in the group move from members to ministers to missionaries, so they move from a self focus to a group focus to an outward focus. They come to see that discipleship is not only about obedience in our personal lives, it's about obedience in expanding God's kingdom in word and deed.

"K" Words

The three "K" words are *kerygma*, *koinonia*, and *kenosis*. *Kerygma* is the Greek word used in the New Testament for preaching. What is the subject of New Testament kerygma? The good news of salvation through Jesus Christ alone.

Once someone believes this good news, they become part of the second word—the *koinonia*. This is the New Testament Greek word used to describe the unique fellowship of the church. This is indeed unique, for the fellowship we enjoy together as the Body of Christ is not because of our background, cultural affinity, race, economic status, or shared interests. Far from these, this koinonia actually bridges the gaps that are among us because of our differences in all the above. But despite these differences, we are bonded together under the grace of Christ, being one new family of faith. As we move from kerygma to koinonia through faith, we find that this new family is eternal in nature and will spend eternity as the coheirs with Jesus.

But again, the group cannot stay here, only relishing the fellowship we have together. We must move toward *kenosis*. This is the word used to describe the self-emptying of our own will, just as Jesus willingly did, not counting His equality with God something to be clung to, but instead humbled Himself to obedient death on the cross (Phil. 2:1-11). Having believed and then having been brought together in faith, we must together practice this kind of emptying as we in big and small ways give our preferences over to the will of God. We don't cling to the way things have always been done, our personal comforts, or even what we like best about the group we've established. Instead, for God's glory, we are willing to give over all those things to see God's kingdom expand in our communities and the world.

Evangelism

The same pattern persists when we look at the evangelistic thrust of a class or a group. The first and most basic thing we can do together is simply to be nice. Be welcoming. Be accommodating. Ask good questions of each other. Follow up with notes and phone calls. This simple politeness and compassion will make us attractive to others.

Soon, a group will find recruiting new people into their group not a chore because their group will be attractive to others. In other words, those outside the group or outside the faith should see something attractive about the Christians in this group. Their love and care for each other should be plainly evident, and desirable.

But niceness and attractiveness only go so far. The group must also be intentional. The old adage says, "Preach the gospel at all times. If necessary, use words." The only problem with that saying is that it's always necessary to use words. No one accidentally becomes a disciple of Jesus Christ. A person only becomes a disciple because of intentional effort empowered by the Holy Spirit. The class, then, must be willing to engage in intentionally gospel-centered conversations with each other that challenge and comfort, that cut and heal.

Conversations

What, then, of the substance of the group? What do our conversations revolve around? At first, it's natural for all these conversations to be "me" centered—what I learned, what I experienced, and what I felt. At this point, the group member is still primarily thinking of the group as an opportunity to receive.

Eventually, the group members stop thinking exclusively in terms of themselves. They begin to see the talents and abilities inside others in the group, recognizing the contribution from the group as a whole. The conversation moves from "me" to "us," as each member begins to consider what the entire group means in his or her life.

But as the group matures, that same group member begins to see that group life is not only about receiving but about giving. The member sees that he or she has unique talents, abilities, and perspective that can shape the faith of others. Then the conversation changes again as that same person begins to consider what their group might do for others. And the cycle starts all over again.

Prayer Requests

If you think back to when you first began to pray, perhaps as a child, you can see the progression happen in your own life. As a child, we all began to pray "me" prayers. We asked God for and about things in our own personal lives. Even as adults, we spend most of the time praying in this same vein.

As adults, and in a group, we begin to pray with others. But because when we first enter into a group we have not really felt the sense of membership, *koinonia*, and belonging that we eventually will, the requests we share are general in nature. But over the course of time, we develop a sense of trust with these people, and those prayer requests become more and more specific.

At the same time, the focus shifts off of ourselves and onto others. We look outside ourselves and begin to pray, really pray, for the needs of those in our group. And then eventually, prayers move outside the group.

This is a healthy progression. But like all the other examples, it doesn't mean we stop praying for ourselves. It only means that we have matured in that process to where we not only look inward, but begin to focus our attention outside ourselves.

"One" Revisited

Ideally, everyone in a church would embrace every one of the points we have discussed. But even if every person does not, you can still grow. There are, however, a few "ones" you cannot do without.

The Pastor

The pastor must be the champion of any intentional effort to take on the 100 barrier. He cannot delegate the load. However, we must share it.

The Sunday School Director

Who is the right person for this role? Is it the person the Nominating Committee talked into it? Maybe for the first time several years ago? A person who has basically functioned as a Sunday School secretary, making sure the attendance rolls are turned in and the quarterly literature order is placed, received, and distributed? Actually, it might be that exact person, if he or she is enthusiastic about leading the charge toward and past 100. The ideal Sunday School Director is the person who has been the most interested, the most animated, the most persuasive among the group who have discussed this book. Chances are, you already know who that is. So who is it?

The Four Age Group Champions

These are the four people who are passionate about one of the age groups. One wants the absolute best experience for adults, and exhorts them to release, reach, and reproduce. Another feels that same passion about students and those who lead middle school and high school kids in Bible study. One believes elementary kids should have at least as memorable an experience as any kid in any mega-church anywhere! She won't be satisfied until you have the capability to use videos and anything else that is available to enhance the discipleship of kids. One who resonates with a hearty amen every time the discussion turns to preschoolers!

The Three Priorities Coaches

These are the people who champion one of the three dimensions of Sunday School. One person cares deeply about teaching. Another is determined to follow up effectively and quickly with all guests. He views every guest as a gift from God, and a stewardship before Him. One gets equally excited when talking about making sure every member is contacted every week; and she is deeply saddened to learn that any need has fallen through the cracks because of a failure to do so.

The Care Group Leaders

One of the secrets of a successful Sunday School is a system of care group leaders. This one assumes responsibility to make a weekly contact with about seven people. If you do nothing else bit that after discussing this book, you will have succeeded.

The Teachers

The Sunday School is nothing without its teachers. These are the ones who arrive early almost every Sunday to lead a class in Bible study. These are the ones who make sure their class is organized to reach and care. These are the ones most likely to exhibit the Ephesians 4 gift of shepherding-teacher or teaching-shepherd. They love teaching the Bible and they love the flock they lead in discovering its grand truths. They are the ones whose memorial service will be said the phrase that needs no explanation: "S/he was a Sunday School teacher."

The Ones Who Do More than One Thing

What if we don't have different individuals to do all of these? It is a blessed church, indeed, that does. Most don't. So what to do? Should we leave the responsibility of champion or coach or care group leader vacant? No. Rather, some people double up. Or triple up. In fact, as you start down the path past 100, I would not be surprised to hear that the Kids champion also covers Preschool, teaches a kids class, serves as the Teaching coach and as a Care Group leader!

Disciples Made One at a Time

Ultimately, we pursue a path past 100 not to get past 100, but to make disciples of more "ones." What if 20,000 churches reached 100 ones each week? What if one did?

Endnotes

1 For more on this concept, see Tom Peters and Robert Waterman, *In Search of Excellence*, (New York: HarperBusiness, 1984).

2 Malcolm Gladwell, *The Tipping Point*, (Boston: Little, Brown and Company: 2000), 179-180.

3 Thom Rainer, *High Expectations*, (Nashville: Broadman and Holman Publishers, 1999), 45.

4 "Seven Traits of Churches with Increasing Per-Member Giving," *Facts & Trends*, Spring 2016, 9.

5 For more on this subject, see Kenneth Haugk, *Antagonists in the Church*, (Minneapolis: Augsburg Publishing House, 1988).

6 Originally proposed in Arthur Flake, *Building a Standard Sunday School*, (Nashville: Baptist Sunday School Board, 1919).

7 Lyman Coleman and Marty Scales, *The Serendipity Training Manual for Groups*, (Denver: Serendipity House, 1989).

8 See Andy Anderson, *The Growth Spirial*, (Nashville: Broadman and Holman Publishers, 1993).

Other Resources by David Francis are available at *LifeWay.com/DavidFrancis.*

Notes and Reflections: